In the Footsteps of Explorers

Henry the Navigator

Prince of Portuguese Exploration

Lisa Ariganello

 Crabtree Publishing Company

www.crabtreebooks.com

Crabtree Publishing Company

www.crabtreebooks.com

Coordinating editor: Ellen Rodger

Series editor: Carrie Gleason

Editors: Rachel Eagen, Adrianna Morganelli, L. Michelle Nielsen

Design and production coordinator: Rosie Gowsell

Cover design, layout, and production assistance: Samara Parent

Scanning technician: Arlene Arch-Wilson

Photo research: Allison Napier

Consultant: Stacy Hasselbacher, Museum Educator, The Mariners' Museum, Newport News, Virginia

Photo Credits: The Art Archive/Marine Museum Lisbon/Dagli Orti: cover; Bridgeman-Giraudon/Art Resource, NY: p. 8; HIP/Art Resource, NY: pp. 6-7; Bildarchiv Preussischer Kulturbesitz/Art Resource, NY: p. 19 (bottom left); British Library, London, UK/The Bridgeman Art Library International: p. 13; Museu de Marinha, Lisbon, Portugal, Giraudon/The Bridgeman Art Library International: p. 25; Private Collection/The Bridgeman Art Library International: p. 30; University of Witwatersrand, Johannesburg, South Africa/The Bridgeman Art Library International: p. 28; Dave Bartruff/Corbis: p. 31; Brooklyn Museum/Corbis: p. 21

(middle); Martin Harvey/Corbis: p. 20; Peter Johnson/Corbis: p. 16; Wolfgang Kaehler/Corbis: p. 18; Anna Peisl/zefa/Corbis: pp. 14-15; Louie Psihoyos/Corbis: p. 24; Dietrich Rose/zefa/Corbis: p. 12; Stapleton Collection/Corbis: p. 5; The British Library/Topham-HIP/The Image Works: p. 10; Mary Evans Picture Library/The Image Works: p. 11; North Wind/North Wind Picture Archives: p. 9, pp. 22-23, p. 26. Other images stock photo CD.

Illustrations: Lauren Fast: p. 4, p. 13 (top)

Cartography: Jim Chernishenko: title page, p. 17

Cover: Prince Henry, wearing brown robes, studies maps of the West African coastline while meeting with explorers in this painting.

Title page: Prince Henry the Navigator sponsored, or paid for, voyages of exploration from Portugal along the coast of West Africa.

Sidebar icon: Some people in the Middle Ages believed that strange sea monsters swallowed ships whole in unknown seas.

Library and Archives Canada Cataloguing in Publication

Ariganello, Lisa
   Henry, the navigator : prince of Portuguese exploration / Lisa Ariganello.

(In the footsteps of explorers)
Includes index.
ISBN-13: 978-0-7787-2433-9 (bound)
ISBN-10: 0-7787-2433-6 (bound)
ISBN-13: 978-0-7787-2469-8 (pbk)
ISBN-10: 0-7787-2469-7 (pbk)

   1. Henry, Infante of Portugal, 1394-1460--Juvenile literature.
2. Explorers--Portugal--Biography--Juvenile literature.
3. Princes--Portugal--Biography--Juvenile literature. 4. Geography, Medieval--Juvenile literature. I. Title. II. Series. III. Series: In the footsteps of explorers.

G286.H5A75 2006   j946.9'02092   C2006-902143-0

Library of Congress Cataloging-in-Publication Data

Ariganello, Lisa.
  Henry the Navigator : prince of Portuguese exploration / written by Lisa Ariganello.
    p. cm. -- (In the footsteps of explorers)
  Includes index.
    ISBN-13: 978-0-7787-2433-9 (rlb)
    ISBN-10: 0-7787-2433-6 (rlb)
    ISBN-13: 978-0-7787-2469-8 (pbk)
    ISBN-10: 0-7787-2469-7 (pbk)
    1. Henry, Infante of Portugal, 1394-1460--Juvenile literature.
2. Explorers--Portugal--Biography--Juvenile literature. 3. Princes
--Portugal--Biography--Juvenile literature. 4. Geography, Medieval
--Juvenile literature.   I. Title. II. Series.
  G286.H5A75 2006
  946.9'02092--dc22
  [B]
                     2006012066

Crabtree Publishing Company

www.crabtreebooks.com   1-800-387-7650

Published in Canada
Crabtree Publishing
616 Welland Ave.
St. Catharines, ON
L2M 5V6

Published in the United States
Crabtree Publishing
PMB16A
350 Fifth Ave., Suite 3308
New York, NY 10118

Published in the United Kingdom
Crabtree Publishing
White Cross Mills
High Town, Lancaster
LA1 4XS

Published in Australia
Crabtree Publishing
386 Mt. Alexander Rd.
Ascot Vale (Melbourne)
VIC 3032

Contents

Into "the Unknown"

Prince Henry the Navigator was a Portuguese prince who lived during a time of European history called the Middle Ages. Thanks to his sponsorship, Portuguese explorers sailed along the west coast of Africa, making accurate maps of the coastline and establishing trade routes and trading forts. His expeditions also led to the first Portuguese colonies.

Navigating Medieval Waters

Before the 1400s, Europeans did not know much about the world outside of their borders. Ocean travel was dangerous, and few explorers had sailed further south than the Equator, a region called "the Unknown." Most people believed sailors' legends that the water near the Equator was so hot that it boiled and that sea monsters swallowed up ships. Medieval European maps showed that most of the world was unmapped and what was mapped was incorrect. Many of these maps were not created for navigation, but as Christian works of art to show how God created Earth. The voyages of Prince Henry's explorers helped break down some of these mental barriers to exploration and make accurate maps for navigation.

(above) Prince Henry was a Christian monk. He belonged to an organization called the Order of Christ, which fought to defend Christian lands against followers of other religions and to spread Christianity.

In the Words of...

On the expeditions that Prince Henry sponsored along the West African coast, Portuguese explorers met different groups of Africans. Prince Henry told his explorers to keep records, called logs, of their voyages. While sailing up the Gambia River in western Africa, explorer Alvise da Cadamosto wrote about his meeting with the Mandinka people.

"They seemed to us to be men who were most handsome of body ... and all wearing cotton shirts. On their head they had a kind of small cap like the Germans wear, except these had on either side protuberances in the shape of wings and in the middle of each cap was a feather, perhaps a sign that they were warriors. [One man] stood in the prow of each canoe bearing on his arm a round shield, apparently of leather ... They hoped to kill us all and then to present everything we had to their lord ..."

(below) Portuguese exploration of Africa had a devastating effect on the peoples of West Africa. Just twenty years after Prince Henry's first expedition, the Portuguese slave trade in Africa began.

- March 4, 1394 -

Prince Henry is born in Portugal.

- 1419 to 1460 -

Prince Henry sponsors expeditions along the west coast of Africa, but does not sail on any of the voyages himself.

- 1460 -

Death of Prince Henry the Navigator.

Medieval Portugal

Portugal lies on the western side of the Iberian Peninsula. In less than a few hundred years, Portugal grew from a small kingdom to become the leader in the Age of Exploration. Prince Henry's expeditions played an important role in this period of European expansion.

The Birth of Portugal

In the 700s, Moors, or Muslims from North Africa, **conquered** the Iberian Peninsula, which today includes the countries of Spain and Portugal. Muslims are followers of the religion of **Islam**. Slowly, European Christians began to push the Muslims out of the Iberian Peninsula in what was called the *Reconquista*, or reconquest. In 1147, the port city of Lisbon was recaptured from the Moors. A short time later, Portugal emerged as an independent kingdom with Lisbon as its capital.

Crusades and Kingdoms

The recapture of Lisbon was aided by Christian soldiers called crusaders, who were on their way to the **Holy Land** to fight the Muslims there. The fighting Christian spirit of the **crusades** greatly influenced Portugal's attitude toward people of other religions during the Age of Exploration. By 1300, Portugal was also defending its borders against other Christian kingdoms of the Iberian Peninsula, such as Castile, which would unite with other kingdoms to form Spain in the 1500s. The Christian kingdoms that had fought to expel the Muslims now fought against each other for land.

Medieval Mediterranean Trade

Trade was important to the Portuguese economy. The Mediterranean Sea lies to the east of Portugal. In the Middle Ages, a great trade in luxury goods flourished there. Goods from the Far East, such as spices and silk, reached the Mediterranean via overland routes through Central Asia that were controlled by **Arab** traders. Ivory and gold, from areas of Africa south of the Equator, called **sub-Saharan** Africa, reached market cities on the North African shores of the Mediterranean. The king and merchants of Portugal wanted to become more involved in this profitable trade.

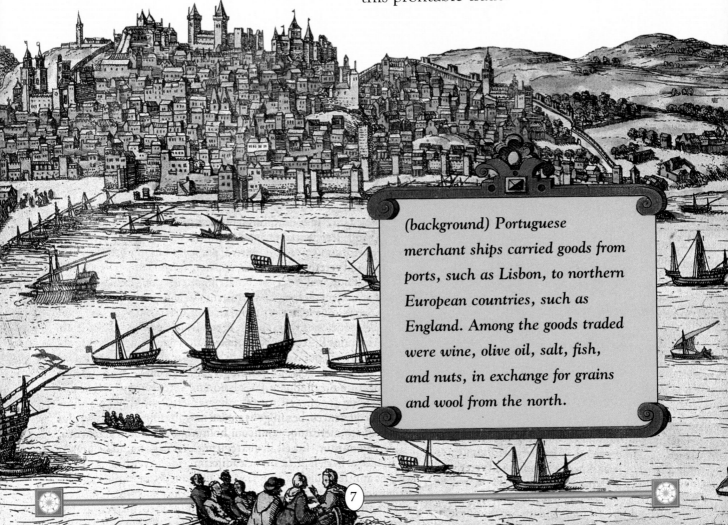

(background) Portuguese merchant ships carried goods from ports, such as Lisbon, to northern European countries, such as England. Among the goods traded were wine, olive oil, salt, fish, and nuts, in exchange for grains and wool from the north.

Royal Beginnings

Prince Henry was the third son of the Portuguese King John I and Queen Philippa from England.

Proving Worth

Henry and his two older brothers, Duarte and Pedro, grew up believing that they had to prove themselves to their father to gain titles, such as a **knighthood**, and land. They also believed in the ideals of the religious crusades, and thought that it was their duty to fight Muslims, as their ancestors had when they reconquered Portugal from the Moors.

(below) The crusades were a series of Christian military campaigns in the Middle Ages to retake the Holy Land from the Muslims.

Attack on Ceuta

In the early 1400s, Ceuta was a Muslim port city in what is now Morocco, in North Africa. North Africa and the Iberian Peninsula are separated by a narrow waterway called the Strait of Gibraltar, which also marks the entrance to the Atlantic Ocean from the Mediterranean Sea.

When he was 21, Prince Henry, along with his brothers, led the Portuguese army in an attack on Ceuta. The Portuguese princes attacked the city to gain glory from defeating a Muslim city, and to be rewarded with titles of honor from their father, the king. Ceuta was a rich prize, where goods from sub-Saharan Africa, such as gold and ivory, were brought and traded. Merchants also traded goods from the East, such as silk and cinnamon, in the city's busy marketplace. Surrounding Ceuta was fertile farmland where grain was grown, and the waters of the Atlantic off the coast could be used for fishing and for looting merchant ships.

(background) Ceuta was a walled city in the Muslim-controlled kingdom of Fez. Inside the city walls, merchants traded goods from both the East and sub-Saharan Africa. In a surprise attack that lasted less than a day, the Portuguese conquered the city.

Lessons from the Conquered City

The Portuguese army succeeded in overtaking Ceuta and the city became the first Portuguese colony in Africa. A colony is land that is ruled by a distant ruler. The king gave Prince Henry the authority to govern the city. While Prince Henry was in Ceuta, he learned about Africa's trade items and geography, including Guinea, a region to the south that was rumored to be rich in gold. To reach Guinea over land meant traveling through the Sahara Desert on Muslim-controlled trade routes. Prince Henry looked instead to the Atlantic Ocean as a possible route to Guinea.

Rewards and Money

When he returned to Portugal after winning Ceuta, Prince Henry was made governor of the Order of Christ. The Order of Christ was a group of military monks that formed to fight against the Muslims. In time, the order grew very rich and powerful. Prince Henry used this money to fund expeditions along the west coast of Africa. Prince Henry's father also made him governor of Algarve, the southern region of Portugal.

Queen Philippa, Prince Henry's mother, died from an infectious disease called the Plague just a few days before the attack on Ceuta.

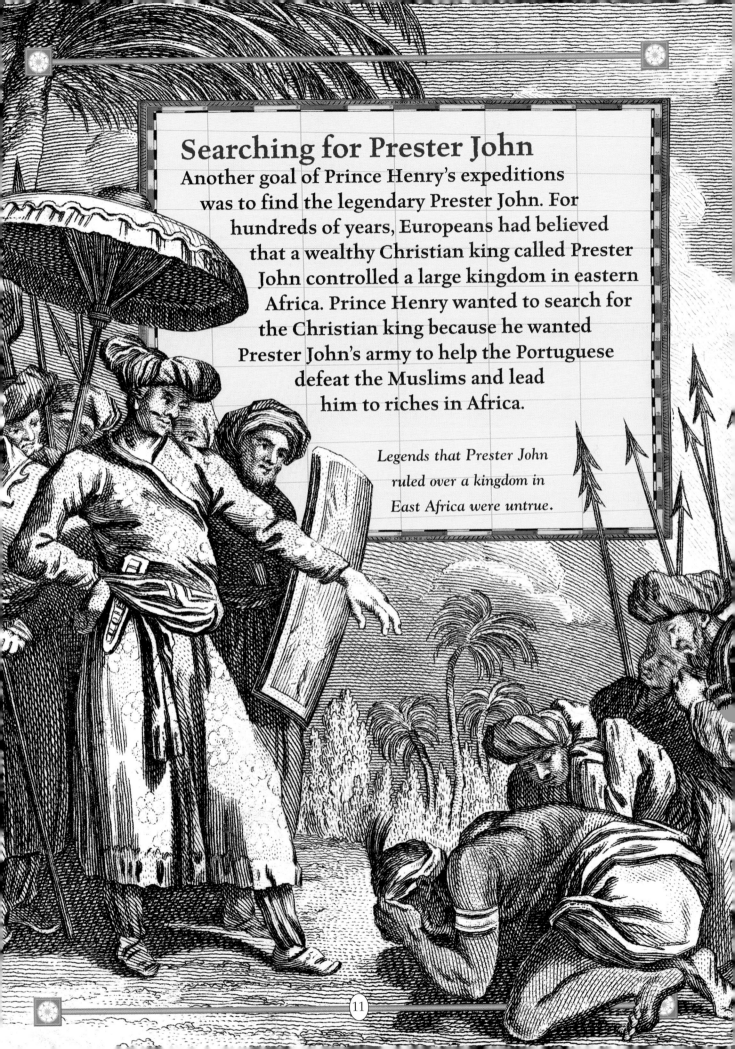

Searching for Prester John

Another goal of Prince Henry's expeditions was to find the legendary Prester John. For hundreds of years, Europeans had believed that a wealthy Christian king called Prester John controlled a large kingdom in eastern Africa. Prince Henry wanted to search for the Christian king because he wanted Prester John's army to help the Portuguese defeat the Muslims and lead him to riches in Africa.

Legends that Prester John ruled over a kingdom in East Africa were untrue.

Island Colonies

Late medieval maps showed many islands scattered about the Atlantic Ocean, or what was then called the "Ocean Sea." Prince Henry sponsored, or paid for, Portuguese explorers to visit the islands. These voyages led to the settlement of Portuguese colonies.

(background) Madeira is the largest island of the Madeira archipelago, in the Atlantic Ocean. The other islands include Porto Santo and two groups of smaller islands.

Island Voyagers

Tristão Vaz Teixeira and João Gonçalves Zarco were two of Prince Henry's **squires**. They sailed to the islands of the Madeira archipelago, a group of islands in the Atlantic Ocean off the coast of present-day Morocco, North Africa. Vaz Teixeira and Zarco returned to Portugal with reports of the uninhabited islands and offers to settle them. Prince Henry was granted permission by his father, King John, to oversee the colonization attempts.

Porto Santo

The first island that was settled was Porto Santo. A Portuguese navigator named Bartolemeu Perestrelo was chosen to lead settlers to the island. Among the animals introduced to the island were cattle and rabbits, which were brought for their meat. The rabbits bred quickly and their population grew out of control because they had no natural **predators** on the island. The settlers soon found that they could not grow food on the island because the rabbits ate their crops too quickly. Instead, the island was used by the Portuguese for fishing, raising cattle, and collecting dragon's blood, a type of tree resin, or sap, that was used in Europe at that time in medicines and for dyeing cloth.

(below) In the Middle Ages, people used plants to make dyes for cloth. Some of the plant dyes were brought from far away.

Bartolemeu Perestrelo was born in Italy but moved to Portugal. He was Christopher Columbus' (above) father-in-law. Columbus is credited with the European discovery of the Americas in 1492. Perestrelo also introduced rabbits (below) to Porto Santo.

Madeira

The largest of the islands, Madeira, was settled by 1425. Vaz Teixeira and Zarco told Prince Henry of the lush forests, fresh water, and fertile soil of Madeira. The island's name, Madeira, comes from the Portuguese word for wood. Immediately after the Portuguese settlers arrived, they started cutting down trees and exporting the wood to Portugal, where it was used to make ships and buildings. Timber was needed in Portugal because it does not have a lot of trees. Crops such as wheat and sugar cane were planted on the cleared land. When King John died in 1433, Prince Henry received lordship of the colonies from his brother, the new king.

Azores Islands

The Azores Islands lay between Portugal and North America in the middle of the Atlantic Ocean. In 1431, Prince Henry sent Frei Gonçalo Vehlo on an expedition to explore the islands, which were known to the Portuguese. Over the next few years, livestock was brought to some of the islands. The animals were brought so that when settlers arrived, they would have a food source. In 1439, Prince Henry received permission from his brother, King Duarte, to colonize the islands. In time, the island colonies produced wheat, fish, sugar, and woad. Woad is a type of blue dye that comes from the woad plant.

Cape Verde Islands

The Cape Verde Islands are located off the west coast of Africa. There were no people living on the islands when the Portuguese landed there in 1456. A few years later, Portuguese settlers arrived on the islands. African slaves were brought to the islands to work on Portuguese plantations. Plantations are large farms that grow one main cash crop. In 1975, Cape Verde gained its independence from Portugal. Today, most Cape Verdeans are of mixed African and European descent.

(background) The Cape Verde Islands were formed long ago by volcanic eruptions. Most of the islands are dry and rocky, and only a few places are suitable for growing crops.

- 1424 -

Beginning of colonization attempts of the Madeira archipelago.

- 1439 -

The Portuguese colonize the Azores Islands.

- 1462 -

Colonization of the Cape Verde Islands begins.

West African Coast

Europeans knew the west coast of Africa only as far as Cape Bojador. Beyond that, they believed stories that strong ocean currents sunk ships and that the hot sun burned sailors alive.

Beyond the Cape

In 1434, Gil Eanes, a squire of Prince Henry, was reported to have sailed past Cape Bojador. He passed the cape and landed on the edge of the Sahara Desert in western Africa. Eanes' return from his voyage reduced some fears of sailing into "the Unknown."

Signs in the Sands

A year later, Eanes made another journey past Cape Bojador with Afonso Gonçalves Baldaya. Just past Cape Bojador, they entered a large bay on the coast of the Western Sahara. Eanes and Baldaya saw human and camel prints near a body of water. This led them to believe that trade was going on through the area and that there was a trading port nearby.

River of Gold

In 1436, Prince Henry again sent a ship to sail even further south along the coast of West Africa. The explorers found and named the Rio de Oro, or "River of Gold." The Portuguese believed that this river led to the source of Africa's gold. The explorers did not find gold on this journey, but they did catch seals and brought the skins and seal oil back to Europe. On this trip, explorer Baldaya mapped over 200 miles (322 kilometers) of the African coastline.

(left) Seal oil was valuable in Europe. It was used for fuel in lamps, for making soap, and for cooking and lubricating oil. Seal oil was made by melting down the blubber, or fat, of seals.

EUROPE

Atlantic Ocean

Portugal

Iberian Peninsula

Mediterranean Sea

• Ceuta

Canary Islands

S A H A R A   D E S E R T

Cape Bojador

Arguin Bank

AFRICA

Senegal River

Gambia River

Cape Verde Islands

S A H E L

Cape Palmas

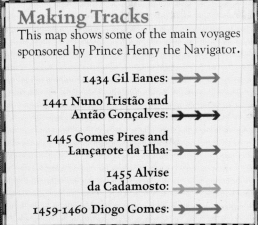

Making Tracks

This map shows some of the main voyages sponsored by Prince Henry the Navigator.

1434 Gil Eanes: →→

1441 Nuno Tristão and Antão Gonçalves: ➤➤➤

1445 Gomes Pires and Lançarote da Ilha: →→→

1455 Alvise da Cadamosto: →→

1459-1460 Diogo Gomes: →→→

- 1434 -

Gil Eanes sails past Cape Bojador.

- 1435 -

Gil Eanes and Afonso Gonçalves Baldaya find footprints near Rio de Oro.

- 1441 -

Nuno Tristão and Antão Gonçalves reach Cape Blanco.

- 1456 -

Alvise da Cadamosto sails up the Gambia River.

- 1459-60 -

Diogo Gomes discovers Cape Palmas.

Islands of the Dry Coast

In 1441, Prince Henry told his explorers to sail further than ever before and bring back everything they could find from the land. Nuno Tristão and Antão Gonçalves sailed down the western coast of Africa and reached the Arguin Bank, off the coast of present-day Mauritania. The islands provided a place for ships to re-stock their fresh water supply, because the West African coast was desert. The sea around the islands was also rich in fish, so the explorers could find more food. When they returned to Portugal, they brought an African prince named Adahu with them.

(background) The coastline of West Africa is mostly desert along what are now the African countries of Western Sahara and Mauritania. The Portuguese explorers risked running short of fresh drinking water and food if they shipwrecked on the coast.

Edge of the Sahara

From Adahu, the Portuguese learned more of the overland trade routes through the Sahara Desert. Many more expeditions sponsored by Prince Henry were sent out. The explorers were looking for items to trade and for people to capture so that they could take them back to Portugal, where they were questioned about the land. Gomes Pires and Lançarote da Ilha are credited with reaching the mouth of the Senegal River in 1445. The Senegal River marked the edge of the desert of West Africa and the beginning of the Sahel, a **semidesert** region. It also marked the end of the area traditionally held by Muslims. To the south were people who held **indigenous** beliefs and led different lifestyles.

(below) From his home in Sagres, Portugal, Prince Henry studied maps and met with explorers bound for West Africa.

Rounding West Africa

During a 1455 voyage to Africa, explorer Alvise da Cadamosto discovered the Gambia River. A year later, on a second trip to the Gambia River, Cadamosto sailed as far as the Geba River, 60 miles (97 kilometers) up the Gambia River into Africa. Cadamosto kept detailed records of the people he met and the information he learned from them about trade in Africa. A few years later, explorer Diogo Gomes sailed beyond the Geba River and visited the town of Kuntaur, Gambia. There, he witnessed the trade of goods from the interior of Africa and met traders from Timbuktu, an important center for learning and trade on the sub-Saharan trade route. Gomes also explored as far along the West African coast as Cape Palmas, in present-day Liberia. This point marked the furthest place in Africa that the voyages sponsored by Prince Henry reached before his death.

(below) The coast of what became the African country of Liberia was called the "Grain Coast." Many cereal crops such as sorghum, millet, and rice grew there.

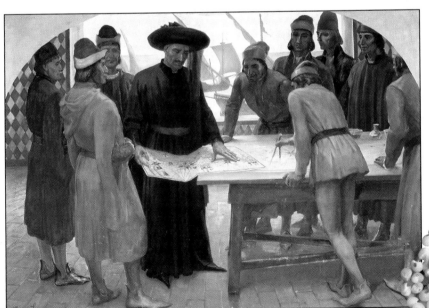

People of West Africa

The west coast of Africa visited by Henry the Navigator's explorers was populated by different ethnic groups. Northwest Africa was home to the Berbers, or Amazigh. They were Muslim traders who bought and sold goods across the Sahara Desert.

Saharan Trade

The Sahara is the largest desert in the world. It stretches across northern Africa. For many centuries, trade across the desert was conducted by camel caravans. In addition to valuable trade items such as animal hides, ostrich eggs, and amber, slaves from areas south of the Sahara were also brought to markets. The Berber people who lived and traded in this area were converted to Islam by Arab invaders in the 700s.

The Tuareg are a Berber group that lived near Timbuktu, in present-day Mali. They were called "Blue Men of the Desert" because they dyed their robes blue.

People of the Sahel

The Sahel is the region south of the Sahara Desert. It has a dry climate and few grassy plants grow there. Many ethnically or culturally different groups live in the Sahel. One of the largest was the Mandinka people. The Mandinka people established the large Mali empire, which lasted from 1235 until the mid-1500s. The Mali empire was rich in gold and salt and prospered from trade.

This wooden carving shows a person playing a traditional instrument called a kora. A kora is a cross between a harp and a lute.

The Wolof

The Wolof people are the largest ethnic group in what is today the West African country of Senegal. The Wolof had many early contacts with Portuguese explorers. The Wolof were ruled by a king and by less powerful chiefs. They also kept slaves, who were either captured in battles or born to existing slaves.

Squire in Africa

In 1444, one of Henry's squires, João Fernandes, lived with a Berber tribe in the Sahara Desert for seven months. Fernandes discovered that the nomadic peoples of West Africa used camels for travel across the desert. Fernandes returned to Prince Henry with reports of African wildlife he saw, including ostriches, gazelles, rabbits, and antelopes. The Portuguese squire also discovered that camels' milk, wheat, and fish were part of the West African diet. Back in Portugal, Fernandes told Prince Henry of an important desert market town called Wadan near the West African coast.

Prince Henry's Slaves

From the earliest of Prince Henry's voyages, explorers were instructed to capture and bring back people from the lands they explored. In Portugal, the captives were questioned about the land, people, and trade of their region. Very quickly, the capture of Africans for questioning grew into a large-scale slave trade.

Early Captives

In 1441, Portuguese explorers captured some of their first African prisoners. Among the eleven people captured was Adahu, who spoke the Arabic language and had traveled the trade routes of the Sahara. Three years later, the first Portuguese expedition solely for the purpose of capturing slaves was made to the Arguin Bank, the same place where Adahu and the others had been captured.

The Prince's Fifth

The expedition was lead by Lançarote da Ilha, but a fifth of the profit made from the sale of the captured Africans was to be paid to Prince Henry. The expedition raided the islands and killed those who resisted. Over 200 slaves were brought back to Portugal, where they were met by Prince Henry and crowds of people. This was the first shipment of slaves from sub-Saharan Africa brought to Europe by Europeans via an Atlantic trade route.

Slave "Factories"

Prince Henry believed that by capturing Africans, selling them into slavery, and converting them to Christianity, he was saving them from Hell. Europeans viewed Africans as inferior because of the ways in which they lived, ate, and worshiped. By 1448, Prince Henry had built a **fortified** trading post, called a *feitoria*, or factory, at Arguin.

(background) As time passed, the demand for slaves rose. Many slaves were caught in village raids, force-marched to the coast, and sold to waiting Portuguese and other European slave traders.

Growing Slave Trade

From there, the population of the Arguin Islands was captured and sold into slavery. Portuguese traders were granted permission from Prince Henry to take part in the slave trade. They made contact with the merchants at Wadan to buy more slaves from the interior of Africa. Slaves quickly became the most important commodity in the Portuguese trade with Africa. Some historians estimate that about 200 slaves per year were brought to Portugal from Africa until 1447. By the 1450s, between 800 and 1,000 African slaves were being brought to Portugal each year.

Caravels and Sailors

Life aboard Prince Henry's caravels was hard for everyone. Crews encountered many difficulties, such as low food supplies, cramped living quarters, unpredictable weather conditions, and diseases. The conditions worsened when caravels were overcrowded with slaves.

Portuguese Caravels

Portuguese explorers traveled in caravels. Caravels during Prince Henry's time were were fast, lightweight sailing craft with **lateen** sails. About twenty crew members and their supplies were carried on each caravel. Caravels could easily sail into the wind and were ideal for exploring the shallow coastal shores and rivers of western Africa.

Coastal Navigation

Traveling into unknown waters was a great risk for European explorers because there were no accurate maps to help them. The rough winds along the west coast of Africa made it difficult to navigate because the winds blew the ships off course. Prince Henry's ships sailed in daylight so they could steer around debris along the coasts.

Slaves were fettered, or chained, at the wrists and ankles, on Portuguese caravels. Some slaves were kept on deck in all kinds of weather, and others were kept below deck in the part of the ship called the hold.

Navigation Methods

- Celestial Navigation -
Celestial navigation was a method explorers used to find their way in the ocean by following the position of the sun, moon, stars, and planets.

- Dead Reckoning -
A navigation method called dead reckoning was used to measure the location of the ship. Distance was calculated by multiplying the ship's speed by the length of time it had been sailing.

(background) Caravels were small ships originally used for fishing by the Spanish and the Portuguese. Over time, as shipbuilding improved, larger caravels were built for journeys of exploration.

Mapmaking

Before Prince Henry's explorers, world maps and charts of western Africa and the Atlantic Ocean were not accurate because European explorers had not traveled beyond Cape Bojador. Scientists and mapmakers speculated, or guessed, as to what was located south of Cape Bojador. New maps were created piece by piece, as the different explorers reached points further along the coast of Africa. Prince Henry's expeditions added nearly 1,500 miles (2,414 kilometers) to medieval maps. These maps helped future explorers to accurately navigate along the coast of West Africa.

Ships' Logs

Prince Henry ordered his ships' captains to keep detailed logs, or journals, of their travels. The logs were descriptions of what they encountered on their journeys. The logs were also an aid for future explorers. The journals of explorer Alvise da Cadamosto were especially important. First published in 1507, his report is the earliest European record of West Africa by a European explorer.

Early maps looked like this ancient map. Prince Henry's expeditions produced accurate maps of the West African coast.

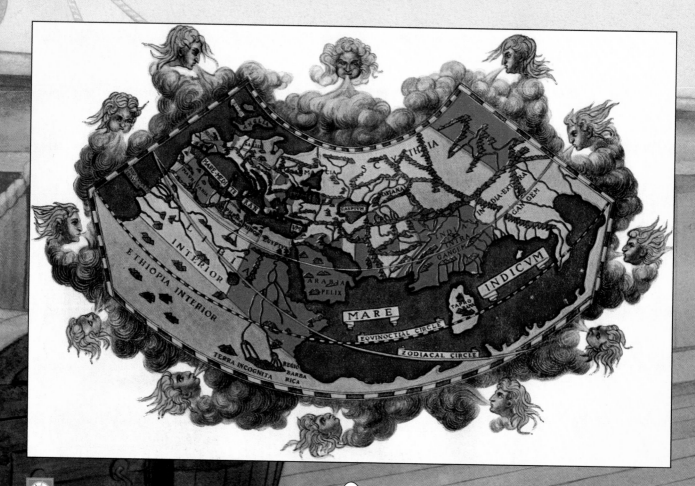

Couscous Salad Recipe

Couscous is a type of pasta made from grain. It is a popular North African dish. Tomatoes and corn were not available in Africa at the time, but have been added here for flavor. Ask an adult to help.

Ingredients:

1 16-oz (454-gram) box of couscous
1 can black beans
1 can whole kernel corn
1-2 tomatoes, diced
1 tbsp (15 mL) cilantro
1/4 cup (59 mL) lime juice

Directions:

1. Cook couscous according to package directions.
2. Transfer couscous into a large bowl.
3. Add remaining ingredients and mix together.
4. Refrigerate for two hours.
5. Serve chilled.

(background) Ship's boys were young boys hired for the voyage. The ship's boys rotated duties, which included leading morning prayers, cleaning the deck, working the sails, serving meals, and pumping out water that collected below the deck.

- Astrolabe-
An astrolabe was a round wooden or brass instrument used to measure latitude, or position north or south of the equator.

- Quadrant -
A quadrant was a triangular object used to measure the height of the stars, from which latitude could then be determined.

- Compass-
The compass was used to determine the direction in which a ship was sailing by reading a magnetic needle that pointed north.

Exploration Continues

After Prince Henry's death in 1460, Europeans continued to explore the west coast of Africa. Prince Henry's great-nephew, King John II of Portugal, took the throne in 1481 and continued Prince Henry's explorations. His goal was to discover a sea route around Africa to India.

Bartolomeu Dias

In 1487, King John II chose Bartolomeu Dias to embark on an exploration down the West African coast. A year later, Dias rounded the southern tip of Africa and sailed into the Indian Ocean. He entered a cape and named it Cabo das Tormentas, meaning Cape of Storms in Portuguese. King John II later renamed it to Cabo da Boa Esperança, or Cape of Good Hope. This discovery was important to European trade because it opened up a direct route to India and the rest of Asia.

Vasco da Gama

Portuguese explorer Vasco da Gama was the first European explorer to sail the direct route from Europe to India. He followed Bartolomeu Dias' route around the Cape of Good Hope and sailed up the eastern coast of Africa to India. This established a new trade route to India that eventually brought great wealth and power to Portugal.

The king of Portugal blessed Vasco da Gama's expedition before it set sail.

Sailing Westward

In 1492, Christopher Columbus, an Italian explorer who was sailing for Spain, landed in the Bahamas and claimed land for Spain. Columbus' discovery caused strife between Spain and Portugal. Portugal had been granted control over newly discovered lands by the leader of the Christian Church. To resolve the dispute, an agreement known as the Treaty of Tordesillas was signed. Under the treaty, Spain was granted lands to the west of an imaginary line on the globe, and Portugal lands to the east. In 1500, Portuguese explorer Pedro Álvares Cabral landed in what is now Brazil and claimed it for Portugal. Portugal sent settlers and crops to Brazil and established sugar cane plantations. Soon after, slaves from Africa began to be shipped across the Atlantic to work on Portugal's Brazilian plantations. The slaves were also sold to colonies ruled by other European nations.

Sugar cane was introduced to Brazil by the Portuguese in 1532. It quickly became the most important crop of the colony. Sugar cane was used to make sugar, molasses, and rum.

- 1488 -
Portuguese explorer Bartolomeu Dias rounds the southern tip of Africa.

- 1492 -
Italian explorer Christopher Columbus reaches the Bahamas.

- 1498 -
Portuguese explorer Vasco da Gama reaches India by sailing around the southern tip of Africa.

- 1500 -
Portuguese explorer Pedro Álvares Cabral claims Brazil for Portugal.

Prince Henry's Legacy

Prince Henry is remembered by some people as the leader of Europe's Age of Exploration. The voyages sponsored by Prince Henry encouraged other Europeans to explore.

Portugal's Wealth

Portugal's early colonies on the Atlantic Islands provided much wealth. In time, sugar cane and other crops and resources were brought to Portugal and sold. Portugal also benefited greatly from the slave trade and set up trade posts along the East Coast of Africa. Thanks to the initial explorations by Prince Henry, Portugal built a trade empire that reached around West to East Africa and eventually to Asia and India.

The Portuguese empire grew to extend into the Pacific Ocean, such as the island of Timor, which Portugal ruled until 1975.

What About Africa?

The slave trade existed in Africa before Portuguese exploration. As other European nations, such as France, England, and the Netherlands, sent explorers to Africa, more slave trade posts were set up and deals were made with African traders to purchase peoples captured from their villages. The biggest market for slaves became European colonies across the Atlantic, including Brazil, where slaves were needed to work on plantations. Almost 10 million Africans are believed to have been taken from Africa as slaves between the 1440s and the 1880s.

Getting the Facts

Historians today debate the role that Prince Henry played in the Age of Exploration. Some historians believe that Prince Henry may have established a "school of navigation" in Sagres, Portugal. Other historians believe that this is a myth. In the past, it was also believed that Prince Henry and his explorers invented the caravel. Historians now know that caravels were used in the Portuguese and Spanish fisheries as early as the 1200s. Much of the firsthand accounts of Prince Henry's life and actions were recorded by the Portuguese royal biographer, Gomes Eanes de Azurara. Azurara wrote an account of the Portuguese explorers of Prince Henry's time called Chronicle of the Discovery and Conquest of Guinea. For many years, this book was used as a primary source of information about Portugal's early explorations in Africa. Many historians now believe that Azurara worshiped Prince Henry as a hero and may have exaggerated the prince's role in the discoveries.

In Portugal, Prince Henry is remembered as a hero. This monument shows Prince Henry and his explorers. It was made to mark the 500th anniversary of the voyages.

Glossary

Age of Exploration A period of European history when Europeans set out to explore new lands and set up colonies overseas

Arab An original inhabitant of the Arabian peninsula

Christian A follower of the teachings of Jesus Christ

colony Land ruled by a distant country

conquer To take over using force

crusades A series of Christian military campaigns in the Middle Ages to retake the Holy Land from the Muslims

ethnic group People with common origin or culture

fortified Protected or strengthened against attacks

Holy Land An area in present-day Israel, Jordan, and Syria that has religious importance for Christians, Muslims, and Jews

indigenous Native to a country or area

Islam A religion with followers that believe in one god and the teachings of the prophet Muhammad. Followers of Islam are called Muslims

knighthood A high social position of the Middle Ages. Knights were soldiers who fought on horseback and were granted land and wealth for their bravery in battle

lateen Triangular sails

medieval Describing the Middle Ages

Middle Ages The period of European history from about 500 A.D. until 1500

monk A male member of a religious community who devotes his life to prayer and study

navigation The science of directing a ship, plane, or other vessel to a destination

predator An animal that hunts another for food

semidesert An area located between a desert and a grassland

sponsorship Paying for or supporting a venture

squire A noble who is in the service of a knight

sub-Saharan Areas of Africa south of the Sahara Desert

Index

Printed in the U.S.A.